Light Meals

LYN RUTHERFORD

MEREHURST

LONDON

Contents

Managing Editor: Janet Illsley
Photographer: David Gill
Designer: Sue Storey
Food Stylist: Lyn Rutherford
Photographic Stylist: Maria Jacques
Typeset by Angel Graphics
Colour separation by Fotographics, UK - Hong Kong
Printed in Italy by New Interlitho S.p.A.

Published 1991 by Merehurst Ltd,
Ferry House, 51/57 Lacy Road, Putney, London SW15 1PR

© Merehurst Ltd

ISBN: 1 85391 144 5 (Cased)
ISBN: 1 85391 240 9 (Paperback)

NOTES

All spoon measures are level: 1 tablespoon = 15ml spoon;
1 teaspoon = 5ml spoon.
Use fresh herbs and freshly ground black pepper unless
otherwise stated.

Introduction

Light, fresh, fast and delicious meals... This exciting recipe collection makes the most of the diverse and exciting array of fresh foodstuffs available from supermarkets, stores and local markets today. The ingredients used are invariably easy to prepare and the cooking methods – fast and simple. The only equipment you'll need is an effective grill, a good non-stick frying pan and a wok for stir-frying. I have a large non-stick wok which has one handle for a good hold, and it is in constant use.

As well as stir-fries and grills, I've included hearty soups that are a meal in themselves; substantial salads and sandwiches; plus a selection of elegant suppers suitable for entertaining. These recipes are ideal for small, spontaneous dinner parties and easy, informal gatherings for lunch, brunch or supper. This casual style is my favourite way of entertaining friends.

Most of the ingredients used throughout the book are available from large supermarkets. Because cooking times are short the emphasis is on quality and freshness. Cuts of meat should be lean and tender, and the vegetables, salads and herbs must be plentiful, bright and fresh. A few items, such as sun-dried tomatoes, preserved artichokes, nut oils and flavoured vinegars will need to be bought from delicatessens. These excellent flavouring ingredients can instantly uplift simple dishes, adding a gourmet touch here and there. It's well worth keeping them as storecupboard basics.

I hope you enjoy my light, fresh, fast and delicious meals: 'Light Meals' for short. It was written for those who, like me, prefer fresh foods to convenience ones but never have enough time for elaborate cooking.

Lyn Rutherford

Spaghetti alle Vongole

A quick, easy pasta lunch or supper, with a Mediterranean flavour. Use fresh plum tomatoes, if possible. If fresh baby clams are not available hunt out jars or cans of clams in shells at your local Italian delicatessen – they make all the difference to this dish.

1kg (2lb) fresh baby clams, scrubbed, or 315g (10oz) can baby clams in shells plus 315g (10oz) can shelled clams
5 tablespoons olive oil
2 cloves garlic, crushed
500g (1lb) tomatoes, skinned and chopped

2 teaspoons tomato purée (paste)
1 tablespoon chopped parsley
salt and pepper
375g (12oz) spaghetti
TO GARNISH:
flat-leaved parsley sprigs

1 If using fresh clams, put them in a large pan with 7 table-spoons water. Cook, covered, over a high heat for 2-3 minutes until the shells open; discard any that remain closed. Strain, reserving the cooking liquid. Remove and discard the shells of half of the clams. If using canned clams, drain both types, reserving 6 tablespoons liquid.

2 Heat the oil in a large saucepan. Add the garlic and fry gently for 3-4 minutes. Stir in the tomatoes, tomato purée (paste) and clam liquid and simmer for 10 minutes. Add the clams and parsley and heat through for 1 minute. Season with salt and pepper to taste.

3 Meanwhile, cook the spaghetti in plenty of boiling salted water for 7-9 minutes or until 'al dente'. Drain thoroughly.

4 To serve, pile the spaghetti into warmed individual serving bowls, add the clam sauce and toss gently to mix. Garnish with parsley. *Serves 4.*

Fish Steaks with Vegetables

This dish is so easy – fish is braised in wine on a bed of vegetables to add flavour and prevent overcooking. You will need a large enough pan to hold the fish steaks in a single layer.

Serve this delicately flavoured dish with buttered new potatoes or a potato gratin.

60g (2oz) butter
375g (12oz) small baby carrots, halved lengthwise
1 fennel bulb, cut into strips
2 small courgettes (zucchini), cut into strips
1 teaspoon finely grated lemon rind
1 tablespoon chopped parsley

4 fish steaks, such as cod, salmon or halibut, each weighing 220g (7oz)
salt and pepper
155ml (5 fl oz/⅔ cup) white or rosé wine
TO GARNISH:
lemon slices
parsley sprigs

1 Melt the butter in a large shallow pan. Add the carrots and fennel and sauté gently for 3 minutes. Stir in the courgettes (zucchini), lemon rind and parsley.

2 Arrange the fish steaks on top of the vegetables, season with salt and pepper and pour over the wine. Cover tightly and simmer for about 10-12 minutes until the fish is opaque and cooked through; do not allow to overcook.

3 Carefully lift the fish steaks on to warmed serving plates and surround with the vegetables. Spoon the wine juices over the fish and garnish with lemon slices and sprigs of parsley. *Serves 4.*

Smoked Salmon & Asparagus Eggs

Serve this extravagant brunch or supper dish with slices of toasted brioche, and with orange juice, white wine or champagne to accompany. You could round off the meal with fresh strawberries and cream.

375g (12oz) thin asparagus spears
185g (6oz) sliced smoked salmon
6 eggs
salt and pepper to taste

15-30g (1/2-1oz) butter
3 tablespoons single (light) cream
TO SERVE:
chervil sprigs to garnish
4 slices brioche, toasted

1 Break off and discard the woody stalk ends of the asparagus and, using a potato peeler, thinly peel the stems. Cut each asparagus spear in half. Cook in boiling water for about 5 minutes until just tender. Drain well and keep hot.

2 Arrange half of the smoked salmon and two thirds of the asparagus on individual serving plates. Roughly chop the remaining salmon and asparagus.

3 Beat the eggs in a bowl. Season with salt and pepper. Melt the butter in a non-stick saucepan over a low heat. Add the eggs and cook, stirring lightly with a wooden spoon, for about 3 minutes, until they begin to thicken and set; take care not to overcook – the eggs should be creamy and soft. Stir in the chopped asparagus, chopped smoked salmon and the cream.

4 Divide the scrambled mixture between the serving plates and serve immediately, garnished with chervil sprigs and accompanied by slices of toasted brioche. *Serves 4.*

Oriental Omelette

4 eggs
15-30g (½-1oz) butter
FILLING:
2 tablespoons oil
1 clove garlic, crushed
1 carrot, cut into thin strips
2 spring onions (green shallots), sliced

90g (3oz) mange tout (snow peas), topped and tailed
6 water chestnuts, chopped
125g (4oz) peeled prawns
handful of coriander leaves
2 teaspoons light soy sauce

1 First prepare the filling. Heat the oil in a non-stick frying pan. Add the garlic, carrot and spring onion (shallot) and stir-fry for 2 minutes. Add the mange tout (snow peas) and cook for 1 minute. Stir in the remaining ingredients and heat through. Transfer to a bowl and keep hot.

2 To make the omelette, beat the eggs with 4 tablespoons water. Melt half the butter in the non-stick frying pan and pour in half of the egg mixture. As the edges of the omelette set, push them towards the centre with a spatula, allowing the runny mixture to fill the pan. Continue cooking in this way until the omelette is just set. Transfer to a warmed plate and repeat with the remaining egg mixture.

3 Divide the stir-fry between the omelettes and serve immediately. *Serves 2.*

HERB OMELETTE WITH MUSHROOM FILLING: To make filling, melt 15g (½oz) butter in a small pan, add 1 halved garlic clove and 1 chopped shallot and cook gently for 2 minutes; discard garlic. Stir in 250g (8oz) sliced mushrooms and cook for 4-5 minutes. Remove from the heat and stir in the cream.

To prepare the omelette, add 2 tablespoons chopped mixed herbs (eg chervil, parsley, chives, tarragon) to the 4 beaten eggs. Make 1 omelette, cooking as above. Spoon filling on to one side of the omelette, fold to enclose filling, cut in half and serve.

Pasta with Parma Ham & Cheese

I recently ate cooked Parma ham for the first time and loved its flavour and papery, crisp texture so much that I could hardly wait to include it in this book! Here I have combined it with some of my other favourites – pasta and sizzling grilled goat's cheese. Offset the richness of this dish with a simple salad.

500g (1lb) paglio e fieno (fine green and white noodles) or spinach and egg tagliatelle
salt and pepper to taste
185g (6oz) Parma ham, cut into ribbons or long wide strips
250g (8oz) goat's cheese, such as montrachet, or crottin de chavignol, sliced

3 tablespoons virgin olive oil
1-2 cloves garlic, crushed
3 tablespoons chopped basil or marjoram
TO GARNISH:
basil or marjoram sprigs

1 Cook the pasta in plenty of boiling salted water for 2-4 minutes or until 'al dente'; drain well.
2 Meanwhile, line the grill pan with aluminium foil and preheat the grill. Arrange the Parma ham and goat's cheese slices on the foil and cook under the preheated grill for 2-3 minutes, until both are browned and sizzling, turning once.
3 Heat the olive oil in a large pan, add the garlic and fry gently for 1 minute. Remove from the heat and add the pasta to the pan, with the chopped basil or marjoram. Season with salt and pepper and toss gently to mix.
4 Divide the pasta between warmed individual serving plates and top each with grilled Parma ham and cheese. Serve immediately, garnished with sprigs of basil or marjoram. *Serves 4.*

Stuffed Aubergines (Eggplants)

Aubergines (eggplants) filled with tomato sauce, mushrooms and coriander make a good lunch or supper on their own, or with a salad. You can prepare them in advance and bake just before serving.

4 small aubergines (eggplants),
halved lengthwise
4 tablespoons virgin olive oil
TOMATO SAUCE:
500ml (16 fl oz/2 cups) passata
1 clove garlic, crushed
1 bay leaf
FILLING:
60g (2oz) butter
1 onion, finely chopped
1 clove garlic, crushed
375g (12oz) button mushrooms,
chopped

30g (1oz) dried ceps (porcini),
soaked in warm water for
20 minutes and chopped
2 tablespoons finely chopped
coriander
salt and pepper to taste
2 tablespoons dried
breadcrumbs
1 tablespoon sesame seeds
(optional)
TO GARNISH:
coriander sprigs

1 First make the tomato sauce. Put all the ingredients in a saucepan, bring to the boil and cook until thickened and reduced by half. Discard the bay leaf. Set aside.

2 Meanwhile, preheat oven to 180C (350F/Gas 4). Scoop out the flesh from the aubergines (eggplants) with a spoon, leaving 1cm (½ inch) thick shells. Finely chop flesh. Arrange the shells in an oiled baking dish, brush insides liberally with oil and bake in the preheated oven for 10 minutes.

3 To make the filling, heat the butter in a large frying pan. Add the onion and garlic and sauté for 3 minutes to soften. Add the chopped aubergine (eggplant) flesh, mushrooms and ceps (porcini); cook for 4-5 minutes until just tender. Stir in the coriander and seasoning.

4 Divide the tomato sauce between the aubergine (eggplant) shells. Cover with the mushroom mixture and sprinkle with breadcrumbs and sesame seeds, if using. Return to the oven and bake for 15 minutes. Serve hot, garnished with coriander. *Serves 4.*

Onion & Three Cheese Pizza

Pizza made with real, fresh dough takes less time to prepare than you might think. This dough only needs to rise once and makes 2 pizzas which will generously serve 4 to 6 people accompanied by a simple salad.

PIZZA DOUGH:
15g (¹/₂ oz) dried yeast
125ml (4 fl oz/¹/₂ cup) warm
* water*
500g (1lb/4 cups) plain flour
good pinch of salt
2 tablespoons olive oil
TOPPING:
45g (1¹/₂oz) butter
2 large onions, sliced

3 tomatoes, skinned and
* chopped*
2 tablespoons chopped basil or
* marjoram*
125g (4oz) Roquefort or other
* blue cheese, crumbled*
125g (4oz) mozzarella, sliced
125g (4oz) red Leicester
* cheese, grated*

1 To prepare the dough, dissolve the yeast in the water in a cup. Sift the flour and salt into a bowl, then stir in the oil and yeast liquid, adding a little extra water if necessary to give a smooth dough. Knead well, then divide in half and roll into two 20cm (8 inch) circles. Place on oiled baking sheets, cover loosely with plastic wrap and leave to rise in a warm place for 20 minutes.

2 Meanwhile, preheat the oven to 200C (400F/Gas 6). Melt the butter in a large frying pan, add the onions and fry gently for 10 minutes.

3 Divide the tomatoes and the onion mixture between the 2 pizza bases. Sprinkle each with basil or marjoram. Arrange the cheeses on top and bake in the preheated oven for 25-30 minutes. *Serves 4-6.*

Ham & Asparagus Gratin

Choose plump green or white asparagus spears for this dish. Serve with new potatoes and a crisp salad garnish.

12 large asparagus spears
6 slices roast ham
30g (1oz/¹/₂ cup) fresh white
 breadcrumbs
30g (1oz/¹/₄ cup) slivered
 almonds

SAUCE:
45g (1¹/₂oz) butter
45g (1¹/₂oz/¹/₃ cup) plain flour
470ml (15 fl oz/1³/₄ cups) milk
90g (3oz) gruyére or mature
 Cheddar cheese
2 teaspoons Dijon mustard
salt and pepper

1 To make the sauce, melt the butter in a small saucepan. Add the flour and cook for 1 minute, stirring. Remove from the heat and gradually stir in the milk. Return to the heat and cook, stirring constantly, to give a smooth sauce. Stir in the cheese and mustard, and season with salt and pepper to taste. Remove from the heat and set aside.

2 Break off and discard the woody ends of the asparagus spears. Using a potato peeler, thinly peel the stems. Cook the asparagus in boiling water for 4 minutes, then drain.

3 Preheat the oven to 190C (375F/Gas 5). Cut the ham slices in half and wrap each piece around an asparagus stem. Arrange the ham and asparagus rolls in a lightly greased baking dish. Spoon over the sauce and sprinkle with the breadcrumbs and almonds. Bake in the preheated oven for about 20 minutes until the sauce is hot and bubbling and the topping is browned and crisp. Serve immediately. *Serves 4.*

Leek & Stilton Soufflé

A successful well-risen soufflé is not as difficult to prepare as many people imagine. Be confident – don't keep nervously opening the oven door – and have a simple green or tomato salad ready and waiting to accompany.

60g (2oz) butter
250g (8oz) leeks, finely chopped
6 teaspoons plain flour
140ml (4½ fl oz/½ cup + 1
  tablespoon) milk

185g (6oz) blue Stilton cheese,
  grated
½ teaspoon powdered mustard
salt and pepper to taste
4 eggs, separated

1 Preheat the oven to 190C (375F/Gas 5). Melt the butter in a saucepan. Add the leeks and sauté over a gentle heat for 2-3 minutes to soften. Stir in the flour and cook for 1 minute, stirring.

2 Remove the pan from the heat and gradually stir in the milk. Return to the heat and bring to the boil, stirring constantly; cook, stirring, until thickened. Stir in the cheese and mustard and season with salt and pepper. Allow to cool slightly, then stir in the egg yolks.

3 Whisk the egg whites until stiff peaks form. Stir a little of the whisked egg whites into the sauce to lighten the mixture, then carefully fold in the remainder.

4 Spoon the mixture into an oiled 1.25 litre (40 fl oz/5 cup) soufflé dish and bake in the centre of the preheated oven for 40-50 minutes, until well risen, golden brown and just firm. Serve immediately. *Serves 4.*

INDIVIDUAL SOUFFLÉS: Divide the soufflé mixture between 4 oiled 315ml (10 fl oz/1¼ cup) individual soufflé dishes. Bake at 190C (375F/Gas 5) for 25 minutes.

Blue Brie & Watercress Tart

Make this tart ahead, if you like, and serve it warm or cold with a leafy salad. You can use a plain creamy Brie if you prefer.

PASTRY:
250g (8oz/2 cups) plain flour
pinch of salt
125g (4oz) butter or margarine
3 tablespoons cold water
  (approximately)
FILLING:
30g (1oz) butter

2 bunches watercress, stalks
  removed
315g (10oz) blue brie, rind
  removed, diced
3 eggs
155ml (5 fl oz/²⁄₃ cup) single
  (light) cream
salt and pepper to taste

1 Preheat oven to 200C (400F/Gas 6). To make the pastry, sift the flour and salt into a large bowl. Rub in the butter or margarine until the mixture resembles breadcrumbs. Add the water and mix to a firm dough.

2 Roll out the pastry on a lightly floured surface and use to line an oiled 20cm (8 inch) flan tin. Prick the base and chill for 15 minutes, then bake blind in the preheated oven for 10-12 minutes. Lower the oven temperature to 180C (350F/Gas 4).

3 Meanwhile prepare the filling. Melt the butter in a large frying pan, add the watercress and cook, stirring, for 1-2 minutes until just wilted. Drain in a sieve, pressing out excess liquid, then arrange in the pastry case. Tuck the brie cubes into the watercress.

4 Beat together the eggs and cream, season with salt and pepper and pour into the flan. Bake in the oven for 30-35 minutes or until set. Serve warm, for preference, or cold, with salad. *Serves 4-6.*

Stuffed Crêpes & Pepper Sauce

To make this dish suitable for vegetarians replace the prawns and lemon juice with 185g (6oz) finely diced mature vegetarian Cheddar. Either use ready prepared crêpes or homemade ones.

8 crêpes
30g (1oz) butter
SAUCE:
1 red pepper, halved and seeded
3 large tomatoes
1-2 cloves garlic (unpeeled)
2 tablespoons virgin olive oil
TO GARNISH:
parsley sprigs

FILLING:
30g (1oz) pine nuts
30g (1oz) butter
1 clove garlic, crushed
2 tablespoons chopped parlsey
500g (1lb) spinach, washed and
  dried
250g (8oz) peeled prawns
2 teaspoons lemon juice
salt and pepper

1 To make the sauce, preheat the grill. Place the pepper halves, skin side up, on a baking sheet and grill, turning, for 10-12 minutes until the skin is browned and well blistered. After 5 minutes, add the tomatoes and garlic and cook in the same way for 5-7 minutes. Peel away the skins of the vegetables and garlic, then purée in a blender or food processor with the olive oil to give a smooth sauce. Set aside.

2 To make the filling, preheat the oven to 190C (375F/ Gas 5). Brown the pine nuts in a large pan over medium heat, stirring constantly; transfer to a plate. Melt the butter in the pan, add the garlic and parsley and cook for 1 minute. Add the spinach and cook, stirring, for 2-3 minutes until just wilted. Squeeze out any excess moisture, then stir in the pine nuts, prawns, lemon juice and seasoning.

3 Divide filling between crêpes and fold to enclose. Use some of the butter to grease an ovenproof dish and arrange the crêpes in the dish in one layer. Dot with remaining butter, cover with foil and bake in the oven for 20 minutes.

4 Just before serving, gently heat the pepper sauce. Serve the crêpes, garnished with parsley and accompanied by the pepper sauce. *Serves 4.*

Mediterranean Kebabs

You can serve these kebabs with pasta or rice, but they are substantial enough with just a salad.

500g (1lb) boneless chicken breasts, skinned
8 cooked Mediterranean (king) prawns
8 bay leaves
2 courgettes (zucchini)
1 yellow pepper

MARINADE:
4 tablespoons olive oil
juice of 1 lemon
1 teaspoon finely grated lemon rind
½ onion, finely chopped
1 clove garlic, crushed
2 teaspoons chopped dill or basil
salt and pepper to taste

1 Mix all the marinade ingredients together in a small bowl.

2 Cut the chicken into bite-size pieces and put in to a bowl with the prawns and bay leaves. Pour over the marinade and leave in the refrigerator for at least 1 hour.

3 Preheat the grill. Lift the chicken, prawns and bay leaves out of the marinade with a slotted spoon, reserving the marinade. Cut the courgettes (zucchini) and yellow pepper into 2.5cm (1 inch) pieces. Thread the courgettes (zucchini), pepper, prawns, bay leaves and chicken alternately on to 4 long skewers.

4 Brush the kebabs liberally with marinade and cook under the hot grill for 7-10 minutes, until the chicken is cooked through, turning once and basting frequently with the marinade. Serve immediately with salad, pasta or rice. *Serves 4.*

Trout with Bacon & Almonds

I love to eat grilled trout with french fries – 'glorified fish and chips' – but for a light lunch or dinner a green salad or vegetable and new potatoes are more appropriate accompaniments.

4 trout, cleaned
juice of ½ lemon
salt and pepper to taste
60g (2oz/½ cup) slivered
  almonds
3 rashers streaky bacon, diced

60g (2oz) butter
1 tablespoon chopped parsley or
  dill
TO GARNISH:
lemon slices

1 Preheat the grill to medium. Using a sharp knife, make 2 or 3 deep slashes in each side of the trout. Sprinkle with lemon juice, salt and pepper. Cook under the preheated grill for about 5 minutes on each side, until tender.

2 Meanwhile, place the almonds in a non-stick frying pan over moderate heat, shaking the pan constantly until the almonds are evenly browned. Transfer to a plate and set aside. Add the bacon to the pan and cook over a high heat for about 3 minutes until crisp. Add the butter and, while it is sizzling, scrape up any bacon residue with a wooden spoon. Stir in the almonds and parsley or dill.

3 Spoon the bacon and almond mixture over the trout and serve garnished with lemon slices. *Serves 4.*

VARIATION: Make a simple stuffing for the trout. Heat 30g (1oz) butter in a small pan and sauté 1 finely chopped leek for 1 minute to soften. Add 2 tablespoons fresh white bread-crumbs, ½ teaspoon grated lemon rind and seasoning to taste. Use to fill the trout cavities before grilling.

Stir-fried Duck with Cucumber

The richness of the duck is balanced by the delicate flavour of the cucumber in this stir-fry. Don't overcook the cucumber or the texture will be totally lost. Serve with plain boiled rice.

500g (1lb) duck breasts, skinned and thinly sliced
1 clove garlic, crushed
2.5cm (1 inch) piece fresh root (green) ginger, grated
4 tablespoons dry sherry
1 teaspoon cornflour
pinch of sugar
3 tablespoons soy sauce
90ml (3 fl oz/¹/₃ cup) chicken stock or water

¹/₂ cucumber
3 tablespoons oil
1 small red pepper, cut into strips
3 spring onions (green shallots), chopped
TO GARNISH:
coriander sprigs

1 Place the duck in a shallow dish. Add the garlic, ginger and sherry, stir and leave to marinate for at least 1 hour.

2 In another bowl, mix together the cornflour, sugar, soy sauce and stock or water. Set aside.

3 Using a canelle knife, remove and discard strips of peel along the length of the cucumber. Cut in half lengthwise and scoop out the seeds. Cut the flesh into 5mm (¼ inch) slices.

4 Heat the oil in a large frying pan or wok. Add the duck mixture and stir-fry over high heat for 3 minutes. Add the red pepper and spring onions (shallots) and stir-fry for 2 minutes. Stir in the cornflour mixture and cook until thickened. Add the cucumber and stir-fry briefly for about 30 seconds until just heated through.

5 Serve immediately, garnished with coriander and accompanied by plain boiled rice. *Serves 4.*

Thai Chicken with Basil

A friend recently returned from Thailand raving about a delicious chicken and basil dish she had consumed large quantities of. I saw the simple idea as a perfect fast supper dish and promptly stole it for inclusion here! It is particularly good served with egg fried rice.

4 boneless chicken breasts,
   skinned
4 tablespoons groundnut or
   olive oil
2 cloves garlic, crushed
2 red chillies, sliced

2 tablespoons light soy sauce
at least 45g (1¹/₂oz) basil leaves
salt and pepper
TO GARNISH:
basil sprigs

1 Cut the chicken into long strips, about 5mm (¼ inch) thick.
2 Heat oil in a wok or large frying pan. Add the garlic and chillies and cook, stirring for 1 minute, without browning. Add the chicken strips and stir-fry over a high heat for 4-5 minutes until cooked through. Stir in the soy sauce.
3 Stir in the basil leaves just before serving and heat through. Season with salt and pepper to taste. Serve immediately, garnished with basil sprigs and accompanied by egg fried rice. *Serves 4.*

VARIATION: Replace the soy sauce with ½ lemon, sliced, plus the juice of ½ lemon and 1 teaspoon soft brown sugar. Stir-fry for 1-2 minutes before adding the basil leaves.

Middle Eastern Lamb Kebabs

Tasty long rissoles of spiced minced lamb are grilled on skewers and served with a light yogurt sauce. Use lean ground beef in place of lamb if you prefer.

KEBABS:
500g (1lb) lean minced lamb
½ onion, grated
1 clove garlic, crushed
1 tablespoon tomato purée
*   (paste)*
2 teaspoons flour
1 tablespoon chopped coriander
*   leaves*
juice of ½ lime
½ teaspoon ground coriander
½ teaspoon ground cumin
½ teaspoon chilli powder
salt and pepper to taste

SAUCE:
155ml 5 fl oz/⅔ cup) thick
*   yogurt*
1 clove garlic, crushed
1 tablespoon chopped mint
TO SERVE:
1 cos lettuce heart, shredded
1 red onion, thinly sliced
4 lime slices, halved
coriander or parsley sprigs to
*   garnish*

1 Put all the ingredients for the kebabs in a bowl and mix thoroughly, using your hands, until smooth and evenly blended. Divide the mixture into 4 portions and carefully shape each portion around a long skewer to make 4 long rissoles. Chill for 1 hour until firm.
2 Meanwhile, prepare the sauce. Mix together the yogurt, garlic and mint in a small bowl and set aside.
3 Preheat the grill to medium hot. Cook the kebabs under the preheated grill, turning frequently, for about 15 minutes, until well browned and cooked right through.
4 Arrange the lettuce, onion and lime slices on individual serving plates. Place a kebab on each plate and spoon over the sauce. Serve immediately, garnished with coriander or parsley. *Serves 4.*

Fillet Steaks with Roquefort

A quickly prepared special occasion meal, served with a crisp salad of frisée (curly endive) and radicchio leaves.

125g (4oz) Roquefort cheese
30g (1oz) butter, softened
2 teaspoons wholegrain
*   mustard*
1/2 teaspoon grated lemon rind
1/2 clove garlic, crushed

1 teaspoon chopped parsley
1 teaspoon chopped chives
4 fillet steaks, each 2.5cm
*   (1 inch) thick*
salt and pepper to taste
parsley sprigs to garnish

1 Using a blender or food processor, blend together the Roquefort, butter, mustard, lemon rind and garlic until smooth. Stir in the herbs and set aside.
2 Preheat the grill. Season the steaks and grill for 6-10 minutes, according to preference, turning once or twice.
3 Spoon the cheese mixture on top of the steaks and serve immediately, garnished with parsley. *Serves 4.*

Marinated Lamb Cutlets

8 lamb cutlets
MARINADE:
75ml (2 1/2 fl oz/1/3 cup) natural
*   yogurt*
2 tablespoons olive oil
juice and grated rind of 1/2 lemon
1 tablespoon clear honey

1/2 clove garlic, crushed
2 teaspoons fennel seeds, lightly
*   crushed*
TO GARNISH:
lemon slices
mint sprigs

1 Mix all the marinade ingredients together in a small bowl. Place the lamb cutlets in a shallow dish and pour the marinade over. Chill for at least 1 hour.
2 Preheat the grill. Remove the cutlets from the marinade and grill for 6-8 minutes, turning and brushing frequently with marinade. Serve immediately, garnished with lemon slices and mint, and accompanied by a salad and minted new potatoes. *Serves 4.*

Madeira Pork with Mange Tout

Slices of pork tenderloin and crisp mange tout (snow peas) are cooked with garlic and flavoured with a delicious Madeira and cream sauce. Serve with new potatoes or pasta.

2 tablespoons oil
185g (6oz) mange tout (snow peas), topped and tailed
30g (1oz) butter
500g (1lb) pork tenderloin, sliced
1 shallot, finely chopped
2 cloves garlic, sliced
125ml (4 fl oz/½ cup) Madeira
4 tablespoons double (thick) cream
salt and pepper
TO GARNISH:
parsley or chervil sprigs

1 Heat 1 tablespoon oil in a large frying pan or wok. Add the mange tout (snow peas) and stir-fry for 1 minute. Transfer to a plate and set aside.

2 Add the remaining oil and the butter to the pan, heat until sizzling, then add the pork, shallot and garlic. Stir-fry for 3 minutes until the pork is sealed on all sides.

3 Add the Madeira to the pan and cook over a high heat for 2-3 minutes until the juices are slightly reduced. Stir in the cream and mange tout (snow peas) and heat through gently. Season with salt and pepper to taste.

4 Serve immediately, garnished with parsley or chervil sprigs, with new potatoes or pasta to accompany. *Serves 4.*

CHICKEN IN WHITE WINE WITH MANGE TOUT: Replace the pork with 500g (1lb) chicken breast fillets, sliced. Use a dry white wine instead of Madeira.

Grilled Radicchio & Chèvre

Choose chèvre (goat's cheese) which has a 'rind' on the outside for this recipe; it will help the cheese keep its shape when melting. Buy artichoke hearts, preserved in oil, from Italian delicatessens. Crusty granary bread is the perfect accompaniment for this light meal.

3 heads radicchio, quartered
4 tablespoons olive oil
salt and pepper
185g (6oz) chèvre (goat's cheese)
  log, sliced
6 preserved artichoke hearts

2 tablespoons capers
2 tablespoons walnut oil
1 tablespoon chopped basil or
  oregano
TO GARNISH:
basil sprigs

1 Preheat the grill. Place the radicchio on a baking sheet, sprinkle with the olive oil and season with salt and pepper to taste. Cook under the preheated grill for 8-10 minutes, turning frequently, until well browned.

2 After 5 minutes of the radicchio cooking time, add the chèvre (goat's cheese) to the grill and cook for 3-5 minutes, until well browned and sizzling.

3 Meanwhile, drain the artichoke hearts.

4 Arrange the radicchio, chèvre (goat's cheese) and artichoke hearts on individual serving plates. Sprinkle with the capers, walnut oil and chopped basil or oregano. Serve immediately, garnished with basil, and accompanied by plenty of crusty granary bread. *Serves 4.*

VARIATION: Try substituting plump heads of chicory (witlof) for the radicchio in this recipe. Like radicchio, chicory (witlof) has a slightly bitter flavour which is mellowed by grilling to delicious effect.

Grilled Vegetables

Simply grilled vegetables are delicious served with garlicky toasted walnut paste and crusty bread. You can make the walnut paste a day or two ahead and keep it covered in the refrigerator. You could also include other vegetables such as aubergine (eggplant), corn cobs and tomatoes.

1 red pepper	*WALNUT PASTE:*
1 yellow pepper	*90g (3oz) walnut pieces*
8 large flat mushrooms	*1 clove garlic, crushed*
6 small courgettes (zucchini),	*1 tablespoon chopped parsley*
halved	*60ml (2 fl oz/¼ cup) walnut oil*
1 tablespoon lemon juice	*60ml (2 fl oz/¼ cup) groundnut*
2 tablespoons olive oil	*or sunflower oil*
salt and pepper to taste	*1-2 teaspoons lemon juice*

1 First prepare the toasted walnut paste. Preheat the grill. Spread the walnuts on a baking sheet and toast for 3-4 minutes, shaking to turn, until dark golden. Place the walnuts, garlic and parsley in a blender or food processor. Process for a few seconds to chop finely, then, with the motor running, slowly pour in the oils to give a paste. Add lemon juice and seasoning. Set aside.

2 Halve and seed the peppers, then cut each half lengthwise into 3 wide strips. Arrange on a baking sheet, skin side up, with the mushrooms and courgettes (zucchini).

3 Mix together the lemon juice and olive oil and use to brush the mushrooms and courgettes (zucchini). Sprinkle the vegetables lightly with salt and pepper. Cook under the preheated grill for 5-10 minutes, rearranging as necessary, until the peppers are browned and blistered and the courgettes (zucchini) and mushrooms are just tender. Transfer the vegetables to a plate as they are cooked and keep warm.

4 Serve the grilled vegetables with toasted walnut paste and chunks of crusty bread. *Serves 4.*

Vegetable & Noodle Stir-Fry

Use a potato peeler to pare long strips of carrot and courgette (zucchini) which are quickly cooked by stir-frying. Prawns or softly scrambled egg may be added at the final stage if you prefer.

220g (7oz) Chinese egg noodles
2 teaspoons sesame oil
3 tablespoons groundnut or sunflower oil
1 clove garlic, crushed
1-2 red chillies, sliced
3 small carrots, pared into strips
3 small courgettes (zucchini), pared into strips
4 spring onions (green shallots), sliced
125g (4oz) small cup mushrooms

125g (4oz) mange tout (snow peas), topped and tailed
2 teaspoons cornflour
125ml (4 fl oz/½ cup) vegetable stock or water
3 tablespoons soy sauce
large pinch of sugar
125g (4oz) short sprouted beans
1 tablespoon snipped chives
1 tablespoon chopped coriander
salt and pepper

1 Cook the noodles in boiling water according to packet instructions. Drain and toss in the sesame oil. Set aside.

2 Heat the groundnut or sunflower oil in a wok or large frying pan. Add the garlic, chillies, carrot and courgette (zucchini) strips and stir-fry for 2 minutes. Stir in the spring onions (shallots), mushrooms and mange tout (snow peas) and continue stir-frying for 1 minute.

3 Blend the cornflour with a little of the stock or water. Add the rest of the stock or water to the wok with the soy sauce and sugar and simmer for 2 minutes. Add the cornflour mixture and cook, stirring, until thickened. Stir in the sprouted beans, chives and coriander and season with salt and pepper to taste.

4 Add the noodles to the wok and stir-fry for 1-2 minutes until heated through. Transfer to a warmed serving dish and serve immediately. *Serves 4.*

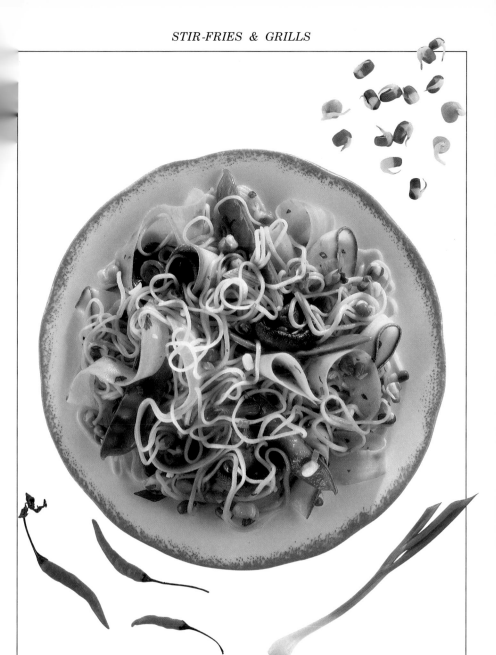

Parsnip & Ginger Soup

Parsnip and ginger is one of my favourite flavour combinations, but you could substitute carrots for all or some of the parsnip. A flavoursome herb bread makes an ideal accompaniment.

45g (1½oz) butter
1 onion, chopped
750g (1½lb) parsnips, chopped
5cm (2 inch) piece fresh root,
    (green) ginger, finely chopped
875ml (28 fl oz/3½ cups) stock,
    preferably chicken
2 tablespoons lemon juice
1 bouquet garni
155ml (5 fl oz/⅔ cup) single
    (light) cream

salt and pepper to taste
HERB BREAD:
60g (2oz) butter, softened
1 clove garlic, crushed
3 tablespoons chopped herbs, eg
    parsley, chives, tarragon,
    chervil, basil, coriander
1 French stick
TO GARNISH:
4-6 tablespoons cream

1 Melt the butter in a large pan. Add the onion, parsnips and ginger and sauté gently for 3 minutes, without browning. Add the stock, lemon juice and bouquet garni. Bring to the boil, cover and simmer for 25-30 minutes until the parsnip is tender. Discard the bouquet garni.

2 Meanwhile, make the herb bread. Preheat the oven to 190C (375F/Gas 5). Mix the butter with the garlic and herbs. Slice the French stick and spread the herb butter evenly on the slices. Reassemble the loaf, wrap in foil and bake in the oven for 15 minutes.

3 Purée the soup in a blender or food processor until smooth. Return to the pan and stir in the cream. Reheat gently and season with salt and pepper to taste.

4 Divide the soup between warmed individual soup plates, garnish with swirls of cream and serve immediately, with the herb bread. *Serves 4-6.*

Tomato & Pasta Soup with Pesto

This is a really simple tomato soup enriched with a pungent spoonful of fresh pesto. Serve with warm bread such as ciabatta, the flat Italian loaf flavoured with oil.

750g (1½lb) ripe tomatoes,
* skinned*
2 celery sticks, chopped
1 carrot, sliced
1 small onion, chopped
1 litre (32 fl oz/4 cups) chicken
* or vegetable stock*
1 tablespoon tomato purée
* (paste)*
1 bay leaf
½ teaspoon sugar
60g (2oz) small pasta shapes
salt and pepper

PESTO:
30g (1oz) basil leaves, finely
* chopped*
3 tablespoons grated Parmesan
* cheese*
1 clove garlic, crushed
30g (1oz) pine nuts, toasted and
* chopped*
4 tablespoons olive oil
TO GARNISH:
basil leaves

1 Place the tomatoes, celery, carrot, onion, stock, tomato purée (paste), bay leaf and sugar in a large pan. Bring to the boil and simmer for 30 minutes. Discard the bay leaf and allow to cool slightly.

2 Transfer the soup to a blender or food processor and work to a purée, then return to the pan and bring back to the boil. Add the pasta to the soup and simmer for 10 minutes. Season with salt and pepper to taste.

3 Meanwhile prepare the pesto. Mix all the ingredients together using a pestle and mortar or a wooden spoon and bowl to give a coarse paste.

4 To serve, ladle the soup into warmed individual serving bowls and add a spoonful of pesto to each. Garnish with basil leaves. *Serves 4-6.*

Black Bean & Vegetable Soup

Cans of preserved black beans are obtainable from Chinese food stores and many supermarkets. They have a superb, but salty, flavour so season this soup with freshly ground pepper only.

60g (2oz) butter
1 onion, chopped
125g (4oz) leek, sliced
2 courgettes (zucchini), sliced
2 carrots, sliced
½ red pepper, halved, seeded and diced
315g (10oz) potato, diced
185g (6oz) French beans, cut into 2.5cm (1 inch) lengths
4 tomatoes, skinned and chopped

1 litre (32 fl oz/4 cups) vegetable or chicken stock
185g (6oz) frozen shelled broad beans, thawed
4-6 tablespoons preserved black beans, rinsed
2 tablespoons chopped coriander leaves
freshly ground black pepper
TO GARNISH:
coriander or parsley sprigs

1 Melt the butter in a large pan. Add the onion, leek, courgettes (zucchini), carrots, red pepper, potato and French beans and sauté for 3-4 minutes. Add the tomatoes and stock. Bring to the boil, then cover and simmer for 25 minutes.

2 Stir in the broad beans and black beans and continue cooking for 3 minutes.

3 Transfer half the soup to a food processor or blender and work to a fairly smooth purée. Return to the pan, stir in the coriander and reheat gently. Season with freshly ground black pepper to taste.

4 Divide the soup between warmed individual serving bowls and garnish with coriander or parsley. *Serves 6.*

Mussel Chowder

A delicious seafood soup, best served with plenty of crusty French bread.

1kg (2lb) mussels in shells
60g (2oz) butter
1 onion, chopped
2 celery sticks, sliced
315g (10oz) potato, diced
2 cloves garlic, crushed
pinch of saffron strands
30g (1oz/¼ cup) flour
500ml (16 fl oz/2 cups) fish or
 vegetable stock
125ml (4 fl oz/½ cup) dry white
 wine

1 bouquet garni
250g (8oz) white fish fillet, eg
 cod or haddock, skinned and
 diced
2 egg yolks
3 tablespoons double (thick)
 cream
2 tablespoons chopped parsley
salt and pepper
TO GARNISH:
parsley sprigs

1 Scrub the mussels thoroughly, removing the beards and discard any mussels that are open.
2 Melt the butter in a large saucepan. Add the onion, celery, potato, garlic and saffron and cook, stirring, for 3 minutes, without browning. Stir in the flour and continue cooking for 1 minute.
3 Gradually add the stock and wine to the pan, stirring all the time. Bring to the boil, then lower the heat and simmer for 5 minutes. Add the bouquet garni, mussels and fish. Cover and cook for about 6 minutes until the fish is tender and the mussel shells have opened. Discard the bouquet garni and any mussels that remain closed.
4 Blend together the egg yolks and cream. Stir a little hot soup into the mixture then remove the soup from the heat and add the blended mixture and chopped parsley. Stir well and season with salt and pepper to taste. Pour into warmed individual bowls and serve immediately, garnished with parsley. *Serves 6.*

Chilli Chicken Soup

A substantial, warming soup of chicken, vegetables and beans flavoured with chilli. Serve with garlic bread or crusty maize bread.

125g (4oz/²⁄₃ cup) red kidney
* beans*
90g (3oz/¹⁄₂ cup) haricot beans
60g (2oz) butter
1 onion, chopped
2 cloves garlic, crushed
4 boneless chicken thighs,
* skinned and chopped*
1 bouquet garni
625ml (20 fl oz/2¹⁄₂ cups)
* chicken stock*
397g (14oz) can chopped
* tomatoes*

1-2 teaspoons chilli powder
2 tablespoons tomato purée
* (paste)*
1 tablespoon Worcestershire
* sauce*
3 sticks celery, sliced
250g (8oz) turnip or swede,
* diced*
2 courgettes (zucchini), sliced
1 tablespoon chopped parsley
salt and pepper

1 Soak the kidney beans and haricot beans in cold water overnight. Drain.

2 Put the soaked beans in a large pan, cover with water and bring to the boil. Boil steadily for 10 minutes, then lower the heat, cover and simmer for 1 hour; top up with more boiling water as necessary. Drain and set aside.

3 Melt the butter in a large pan. Add the onion, garlic and chicken and sauté for 5 minutes. Add the bouquet garni, stock, tomatoes, chilli powder, tomato purée (paste), Worcester sauce, and vegetables. Stir well and bring to the boil. Cover and simmer for 25 minutes, until the vegetables are tender.

4 Discard the bouquet garni. Stir the parsley and beans into the soup, reheat and season with salt and pepper to taste. Serve hot. *Serves 6.*

Spiced Lamb & Coconut Soup

Flavours of Malaysia – provided by lemon grass, chilli, coconut and spices – make this an unusual main course soup.

750g (1½lb) neck of lamb
1 clove garlic, crushed
2 bay leaves
1 stalk lemon grass
1 green chilli, halved and
*   seeded*
2 teaspoons coriander seeds,
*   lightly crushed*
1 teaspoon cumin seeds, lightly
*   crushed*
1 teaspoon garam masala
1 litre (32 fl oz/4 cups) stock or
*   water*

125g (4oz/²/₃cup) red lentils
60g (2oz) creamed coconut
1 onion, chopped
2 large carrots, grated
250g (8oz) potato, diced
2 sticks celery, sliced
125g (4oz) sweetcorn kernels
salt and pepper
TO GARNISH:
toasted coconut
coriander or parsley sprigs

1 Trim the lamb and remove the fat. Place in a large pan with the garlic, bay leaves, lemon grass, chilli and spices. Add the stock or water, bring to the boil, then cover and simmer for 1½ hours, skimming occasionally. Discard the bay leaves, lemon grass and chilli.

2 Using a slotted spoon, remove the meat from the pan and set aside. Add the lentils, coconut and vegetables to the pan. Bring to the boil and simmer for 30 minutes, until the lentils and vegetables are tender. Transfer half of the soup to a food processor or blender and work to a purée. Return to the pan.

3 Remove the lamb from the bone, cut into 2.5cm (1 inch) pieces and add to the soup. Reheat and simmer for a further 5 minutes. Season with salt and pepper to taste. Serve hot, sprinkled with toasted coconut and garnished with coriander or parsley. *Serves 6.*

Classic Club Sandwich

A three layer sandwich of smoked chicken, roast ham and salad.
Eat it the American way – with a generous salad garnish.

*250g (8oz) smoked chicken,
  chopped
2 spring onions (green shallots),
  chopped
3 tablespoons mayonnaise
salt and pepper
75g (2½oz) butter
16 slices brown or white bread*

*wholegrain mustard to taste
8 slices roast ham
4 tomatoes, thinly sliced
about 60g (2oz) salad leaves
TO GARNISH:
lemon slices
mixed salad leaves
few radishes*

1 In a small bowl, mix together the smoked chicken, spring
onions (green shallots) and mayonnaise. Season with salt
and pepper to taste.
2 Thinly butter each slice of bread on one side only. Place 4
slices, buttered side up, on a board. Spread with mustard to
taste, then place a slice of roast ham on each. Divide half of
the tomato slices and salad leaves between the bread slices,
then add another layer of bread.
3 Divide the smoked chicken mixture between the sandwiches and top with another layer of bread. Spread with
mustard and cover with the remaining ham, tomato and
salad. Top with the final bread slices. Secure the sandwiches
with cocktail sticks then cut into quarters. Serve garnished
with lemon slices, mixed salad leaves and radishes.
Serves 4-6.

BACON, LETTUCE AND TOMATO SANDWICH 'BLT': Replace the
smoked chicken filling with 8 rashers crispy grilled streaky
bacon and 2 sliced tomatoes. In place of the ham and
mustard, use 3 chopped hard-boiled eggs mixed with 3 tablespoons mayonnaise.

New York Bagels

Whatever you fill bagels with, it's well worth warming them for a few minutes in the oven first. Each of the filling recipes here will generously fill 2 bagels. You can, of course, simply double up either filling to fill all 4 bagels.

4 bagels
HERRING & EGG FILLING:
2 eggs, hard-boiled and chopped
3 tablespoons mayonnaise
2 teaspoons chopped parsley
salt and pepper
2 roll-mop herrings, sliced
few small parsley sprigs

SMOKED SALMON FILLING:
125g (4oz) cream cheese
2 teaspoons snipped chives
2 teaspoons lemon juice
freshly ground black pepper
60g (2oz) smoked salmon slices
TO GARNISH:
lemon slices
chives
salad leaves

1 Preheat the oven to 180C (350F/Gas 4). Warm the bagels in the oven for 5 minutes, then cut in half horizontally.
2 To prepare the herring and egg filling, in a small bowl mix together the chopped eggs, mayonnaise and parsley. Season with salt and pepper to taste. Divide the egg mixture between 2 bagel bases. Slice the roll-mops and arrange on top of the egg, with parsley sprigs. Replace the bagel tops.
3 To prepare the smoked salmon filling, in a small bowl mix together the cream cheese, chives and lemon juice. Season with pepper to taste. Divide the cream cheese mixture between the remaining 2 bagel bases and arrange the smoked salmon on top. Replace the bagel tops.
4 Serve the bagels garnished with lemon slices, chives and salad leaves. *Serves 4.*

Brunch Muffins

4 large flat mushrooms
2 tablespoons oil
salt and pepper to taste
8 rashers streaky bacon
4 wholemeal muffins, split

5 eggs
4 tablespoons creamy milk
2 teaspoons snipped chives
45g (1½oz) butter

1 Preheat the grill. Brush mushrooms lightly with oil and sprinkle with salt and pepper. Place on a baking sheet with the bacon. Grill, turning once, until cooked. Keep warm.
2 Lightly toast the muffins on both sides. Keep warm.
3 Beat together the eggs, milk and chives. Melt the butter in a non-stick saucepan, add the egg mixture and cook, stirring, for 3-4 minutes to softly scramble.
4 Sandwich each muffin together with 2 bacon rashers, a grilled mushroom and a portion of scrambled egg. Serve immediately. *Serves 2-4.*

Pain Bagnat

This version of a traditional Provencal snack is made with tomato, onion, basil and brie. The bread must be 'bathed' in olive oil.

4 short French sticks or large
   crusty rolls
125ml (4 fl oz/1 cup) virgin olive
   oil
1 clove garlic, crushed
salt and pepper to taste

4 large tomatoes, thinly sliced
1 onion, thinly sliced
315g (10oz) brie, thinly sliced
3 tablespoons chopped basil
6 black olives, stoned and sliced

1 Preheat the oven to 180C (350F/Gas 4). Cut the bread in half horizontally and sprinkle the cut sides with the olive oil, garlic, salt and pepper. Reassemble the loaves or rolls and place on a baking sheet. Bake in the oven for about 5 minutes until warmed.
2 Fill the French sticks or rolls with the tomatoes, onion, brie, basil and olives. Serve immediately. *Serves 4.*

Muffins Florentine

Toasted muffins – topped with spinach in a creamy mustard sauce and softly poached eggs – make a perfect brunch or fast supper.

4 muffins
4 eggs
2 tablespoons vinegar (optional)
30g (1oz) butter
375g (12oz) spinach leaves,
  shredded
90ml (3 fl oz/¹⁄₃ cup) double
  (thick) cream

2-3 teaspoons wholegrain
  mustard
2 teaspoons chopped parsley
salt and pepper
TO GARNISH:
paprika for sprinkling
parsley sprigs
stuffed green olives

1 Split the muffins and toast on both sides. Keep warm.
2 Cook the eggs in a poaching pan over hot water, for about 4 minutes. Alternatively pour water into a large saucepan to a depth of 5cm (2 inches). Add the vinegar and bring to the boil, then lower the heat to a gentle simmer. Crack an egg on to a saucer and gently slide into the pan. Repeat with another egg. Cook 2 eggs at a time for 3-4 minutes until softly set. Set aside and keep warm while cooking the other 2 eggs.
3 Melt the butter in a saucepan, add the spinach and cook, stirring, for 1-2 minutes until just wilted. Drain off any excess liquid, then stir in the cream, mustard and parsley. Heat through for a few seconds and season with salt and pepper to taste.
4 To serve, arrange 2 muffin halves on each individual serving plate, and spoon over the creamed spinach. Top each serving with a poached egg and sprinkle with paprika. Serve immediately, garnished with parsley sprigs and stuffed olives. *Serves 4.*

Summer Salad with Herb Toasts

Be generous with the garlic and fresh herbs used to make the hot little toasts that provide the perfect contrast to a crisp, fresh summer salad.

250g (8oz) asparagus spears
90g (3oz) mange tout (snow peas)
1 cos lettuce
½ head frisée (curly endive)
1 stick celery, cut into fine julienne
1 courgette (zucchini), cut into fine julienne
12 cherry tomatoes, halved
DRESSING:
4 tablespoons olive or nut oil

2 tablespoons white wine vinegar
pinch of salt
salt and pepper to taste
HERB TOASTS:
1 thin French stick
60g (2oz) butter, softened
1 tablespoon ground almonds
2 cloves garlic, crushed
3 tablespoons chopped mixed herbs, eg basil, tarragon, parsley, marjoram, chives

1 Break off and discard the woody ends of the asparagus. Peel the stalks and cut each spear in half. Cook in boiling water for 4-5 minutes only, then refresh with cold water, drain and allow to cool. Blanch the mange tout (snow peas) in boiling water for 1 minute, refresh and cool as above.

2 Tear the cos lettuce and frisée (endive) into bite-size pieces and place in a bowl with the asparagus, mange tout (snow peas), celery, courgette (zucchini) and tomatoes. Cover and chill until required.

3 To make the dressing, mix all the ingredients together in a small bowl or shake in a screw-top jar to combine.

4 For the herb toasts, cut the French stick into 2.5cm (1 inch) slices. In a bowl, blend together the butter, ground almonds, garlic and herbs.

5 Just before serving, preheat the grill and toast the bread until golden on both sides. Divide the garlic and herb butter between the hot toasts. Flash under the grill for a few seconds to heat through. Pour the dressing over the salad, toss lightly and serve with the herb toasts. *Serves 4.*

Rosti & Salad

A light, fresh salad enhanced by a walnut oil dressing is served on top of a hot, crisp potato cake.

ROSTI:
1kg (2lb) potatoes, peeled
3 tablespoons olive oil
1 small onion, finely chopped
salt and pepper to taste
30g (1oz) butter
SALAD:
about 185g (6oz) mixed salad
  leaves, eg frisée (curly endive),
  lamb's lettuce (corn salad),
  chicory (witlof)
125g (4oz) carrot, cut into
  julienne strips
1 courgette (zucchini), cut into
  julienne strips
2 teaspoons chopped parsley or
  chervil
DRESSING:
2 tablespoons olive oil
2 tablespoons walnut oil
2 tablespoons wine vinegar
1/2 teaspoon French mustard
1/2 teaspoon sugar
salt and pepper to taste
TO GARNISH:
parsley or chervil sprigs

1 Partially cook the potatoes in boiling salted water for about 8 minutes. Drain and allow to cool.

2 Meanwhile heat 1 tablespoon oil in a medium frying pan. Add the onion and cook gently for 3 minutes until softened but not browned. Coarsely grate the potatoes into a large bowl. Add the onion and seasoning; mix well.

3 To prepare the salad, combine the salad leaves, carrot, courgette (zucchini) and herbs in a large bowl; cover and chill until required. Mix the dressing ingredients together in a small bowl or shake in a screw-top jar to combine.

4 To prepare the rosti, divide the potato mixture into 4 portions. Heat 1/2 tablespoon olive oil and a little butter in the frying pan until hot and sizzling. Add a potato portion to the pan and flatten firmly to form a 'cake'. Cook over a medium heat for 8-10 minutes, turning once, until golden. Transfer to a plate and keep hot while preparing the others. Repeat to make 4 rosti.

5 To serve, place the rosti on individual serving plates. Add the dressing to the salad, toss well and pile on to the rosti. Serve immediately, garnished with herbs. *Serves 4.*

Crab Salad

For a more elaborate meal you can, if you like, include other seafood in this salad, such as prawns, mussels or sliced scallops. However, I think it is delicious just as it is, served with slices of crusty brown bread or a basket of freshly made melba toast.

1 large cooked crab, weighing about 1.25kg (2½lb)
2 tablespoons mayonnaise
1 tablespoon single (light) cream
2 tablespoons lemon juice
salt and pepper
125g (4oz) salad leaves, eg red oakleaf, frisée, (curly endive) roquette, lamb's lettuce (corn salad)
1 box mustard and cress

small handful of chervil sprigs or snipped chives
8 cherry tomatoes, halved
DRESSING:
2 tablespoons grapeseed or light olive oil
2 teaspoons white wine vinegar
½ teaspoon grated lemon rind
pinch of sugar
salt and pepper to taste
TO GARNISH:
lemon wedges

1 Carefully remove the white and dark meat from the crab claws, legs and carcass, discarding the feathery gills and dead man's fingers. Place the crab meat in a bowl. Add the mayonnaise, cream, lemon juice and salt and pepper to taste. Stir lightly until evenly blended. Set aside.
2 Place the salad leaves, mustard and cress, herbs and tomatoes in a separate bowl.
3 To make the dressing, stir all the ingredients together in a small bowl or shake in a screw-top jar to combine.
4 Pour the dressing over the leafy salad and toss gently to mix. Divide between individual serving plates, pile the crab mixture into the centre and garnish with lemon wedges.
Serves 4.

Prawn, Rice & Avocado Salad

A dash of Pernod gives this dressing an extra lift and goes particularly well with the prawns. If you prefer not to use it add a teaspoon of creamed horseradish to the dressing instead.

125g (4oz) mange tout (snow peas)
185g (6oz/1 cup) cooked white rice
250g (8oz) large peeled prawns
½ yellow pepper, diced
2 spring onions (green shallots), shredded
2 avocados

DRESSING:
3 tablespoons mayonnaise
2 tablespoons natural yogurt or cream
1-2 tablespoons chopped dill
2 tablespoons Pernod or anisette
salt and pepper to taste
TO GARNISH:
1 'little Gem' lettuce heart
few red oakleaf lettuce leaves
few mint or fennel leaves

1 Mix all the dressing ingredients together in a small bowl and set aside.
2 Blanch the mange tout (snow peas) in boiling water for 1 minute, then refresh with cold water and drain well. Place in a large bowl with the rice, prawns, yellow pepper and spring onions (shallots). Halve, stone and peel the avocados, then chop and add to the salad. Add 2 tablespoons of the dressing and toss lightly to mix.
3 Divide the rice salad between individual serving bowls. Garnish with the lettuce leaves and herbs. Serve the remaining dressing separately. *Serves 4.*

VARIATION: Serve this salad in the scooped-out avocado shells as an attractive starter. Reduce the quantity of rice to 125g (4oz/⅔ cup).

Roll-Mops with Apple

This salad makes a tasty lunch served with new potatoes or pumpernickel bread.

8 roll-mop herrings, halved
½ red oakleaf lettuce
2 spring onions (green shallots),
    sliced
1 red apple, cored, halved and
    thinly sliced
2 sticks celery, sliced

DRESSING:
4 tablespoons soured cream or
    natural yogurt
2 tablespoons mayonnaise
1 teaspoon lemon juice
pinch of sugar
salt and pepper to taste
TO GARNISH:
pinch of paprika

1 Arrange the roll-mops, lettuce, spring onions (shallots), apple and celery on individual serving plates.
2 To make the dressing, stir all the ingredients together in a small bowl. Spoon over the salad and sprinkle with paprika to serve. *Serves 4.*

Spinach, Egg & Salami Salad

500g (1lb) young spinach leaves
½ red onion, thinly sliced
60g (2oz) Milano or other
    salami, thinly sliced
4 eggs, hard-boiled and sliced

DRESSING:
30g (1oz) pine nuts
5 tablespoons olive oil
1 clove garlic, crushed
2 tablespoons red wine vinegar
½ teaspoon French mustard
salt and pepper

1 Wash and dry the spinach thoroughly, tear into bite-sized pieces and place in a bowl with the onion, salami and eggs.
2 Lightly brown the pine nuts in a small frying pan over a medium heat. Add the olive oil, garlic, vinegar and mustard. When the dressing is hot, season with salt and lots of pepper and pour over the salad. Toss gently and serve immediately. *Serves 4.*   *(Illustrated on page 1)*

Hot Chicken & Roquette Salad

I love meals like this which are quickly cooked and can be eaten with just a fork, casually among friends. Wash it down with large glasses of Sancerre or Sauvignon wine!

125g (4oz) French beans, topped and tailed
250g (8oz) roquette
1 small onion, thinly sliced
4-6 tablespoons olive or groundnut oil
3 boneless chicken breasts, sliced

60g (2oz/²⁄₃ cup) walnut halves
1-2 cloves garlic, crushed
2 teaspoons shredded lemon rind
juice of 1 lemon
1 teaspoon brown sugar
salt and pepper
chopped parsley to garnish (optional)

1 Cook the French beans in boiling water for 2 minutes only. Refresh with cold water, drain and set aside. Arrange a bed of roquette and onion rings on 4 individual serving plates.

2 Heat 4 tablespoons oil in a wok or large frying pan. Add the chicken and stir-fry over a high heat for about 4 minutes until lightly browned. Add the walnuts and garlic and continue stir-frying for 2-3 minutes, adding more oil if necessary, until the chicken is cooked through.

3 Add the lemon rind and juice to the pan, together with the sugar and French beans. Continue cooking for 1 minute to heat through, then season with salt and pepper to taste. Spoon over the roquette and onion and serve immediately, sprinkled with chopped parsley if desired. *Serves 4.*

VARIATION: Replace the walnut halves with blanched almonds and use orange rind and juice instead of lemon.

Lamb Salad with Mint Dressing

Use pink, tender cooked lamb in this salad. Serve it with tiny new potatoes and a glass of Beaujolais for a refreshing summer lunch.

1 cos lettuce
½ cucumber
170g (6oz) can pimento, drained
and sliced
2 ripe pears, halved, cored and
sliced
4 spring onions (green shallots),
shredded
375g (12oz) cold roast lamb

DRESSING:
150g (5.3oz) carton natural
yogurt
2 teaspoons finely chopped mint
½ teaspoon clear honey
salt and pepper
TO GARNISH:
mint sprigs

1 Tear the cos lettuce into bite-size pieces and arrange on individual serving plates. Using a canelle knife, remove strips of peel along the length of the cucumber, then slice thinly. Add to the lettuce with the pimento, pear slices and spring onion (shallot).
2 Slice the lamb into thin strips and arrange on top of the individual salads.
3 Mix the dressing ingredients together in a small bowl. Drizzle the dressing over the salad. Garnish with mint sprigs to serve. *Serves 4.*

LAMB AND FETA SALAD: Replace the pears with 125g (4oz) Feta cheese, crumbled. Instead of the yogurt dressing, use a vinaigrette: mix together 4 tablespoons virgin olive oil; 2 tablespoons white wine vinegar; ½ clove garlic, crushed; 1 teaspoon clear honey; 2 teaspoons finely chopped mint.

Index